book belongs to this book

Advance Praise for
A Very Special Episode

"Television was a childhood companion for many of us, and the loving, sometimes complicated, investment we put into those characters comes through in *A Very Special Episode*. dueck plays with formal construction and forms that allude specifically and often hilariously to poems from the canon. But these poems are about cartoons and wrestling and commercials and *Care Bears*. Attuned to the specific relevance, joy and pervasiveness of the pop culture that is our culture this collection shows us the ways these trademarks are imprinted on us, are a part of home. As a result we must ask ourselves what it means. Laughs! Games! Serious contemplation! This collection has it all. This book is a delight."

– Dina Del Bucchia, author of *It's a Big Deal!*

"Language is a cult. Pop culture is a language. And here dueck is a cult-leading pop-culture language mixmaster, fashioning poems bright as TV, casting strange and true shadows over our real and hyperreal bodies, illuminating our world with its uncanny undulations and strange flashes. He knows that life is the ultimate in binge-watching. So are our brains. dueck's poems broadcast on all the channels at once, channelling and challenging with technical finesse and flash. He's embedded himself in the broadband of the now, streaming his incisive and witty 5G reports from inside the contemporary ever-flickering dream machine, the motherboard of all our best and most notorious fantasies."

– Gary Barwin, author of *No TV for Woodpeckers*

"nathan dueck takes nostalgic faves like *DuckTales*, *Pac-Man* and the greatest invention of our time – the ThighMaster – and twist/turns them into playful works that slide off the tongue. Like looking at a time capsule of pop culture through a kaleidoscope, this book is a reminder that poetry can be fun like Saturday morning cartoons."

– Daniel Zomparelli, author of *Everything Is Awful and You're a Terrible Person*

A VERY SPECIAL **EPISODE**

Also by nathan dueck

he'll

king's(mère)

A Very Special Episode

A Buckrider Book

brought to you by
nathan dueck

Buckrider Books is an imprint of Wolsak and Wynn Publishers.

Cover and interior design: Jared Shapiro
Author photograph on back cover: Wess Freeheart
Author photograph on page 109: Jostens Canada
Typeset in Lora, and using other licensed or public domain fonts
Printed by Coach House Printing Company Toronto, Canada

23   22   21   20   19   1   2   3   4   5

The publisher gratefully acknowledges the support of the Ontario Arts Council, the Canada Council for the Arts and the Government of Canada.

Buckrider Books
280 James Street North
Hamilton, ON
Canada L8R 2L3

Library and Archives Canada Cataloguing in Publication

Title: A very special episode / brought to you by Nathan Dueck.
Names: Dueck, Nathan, 1979- author.
Description: Poems.
Identifiers: Canadiana 20190160977 | ISBN 9781928088943 (softcover)
Classification: LCC PS8557.U28145 V47 2019 | DDC C811/.6—dc23

for Cal-El,
who has great powers

<PRESS ANY KEY TO CONTINUE>█

```
c:\Users\reader\pop-cult\a-very-special-episode\Table_0f_Contents>cd..
c:\Users\reader\pop-cult\a-very-special-episode>read-me
<INVALID SYNTAX>
c:\Users\reader\pop-cult\a-very-special-episode>begin
<INVALID SYNTAX>
c:\Users\reader\pop-cult\a-very-special-episode>Excelsior?
<INVALID SYNTAX>
c:\Users\reader\pop-cult\a-very-special-episode>run
<RUNNING PR0GRAM: a-very-special-episode>
```

Did you hear Astro Boy®s error
In his report to the computer
Geronimo? Is your heart true or
Do you fear Astro Boy®s error?
Is he a Frankenstein creature or
The Tin Woodsman? Is his chest barer?
Will you share Astro Boy®s error
In your review on a computer?

ON PANELS WITH POMEGRANATES AND INSTRUMENTS OF MUSIC

Now one of the mistranslated passages said: "Kal-El™ trod upon fire
Without blemish. From a pillar of cloud on the mount,
From silver trumpet's noise, the Tetragrammaton° arises: the desert."
Therefore Jimmy bowed down his head and fell to the ground: "The stranger
From a strange land has entered into the House of El." He wiped
His pale cheeks' freckled spots as he had forgotten manna

And made petition of Kara for an omer of manna.
"O man," she interceded, "the skies are adorned with fire
This day, so thou must not tarry long." She wiped
Out the golden pot and lifted up her eyes. The mount
Seemed to stretch higher. "Without doubt the stranger
Born on Krypton™ shall lead us all through this wilderness of desert."

Verily they had not forgotten milk and honey in the desert.
Kara was examining some cakes to pluck out worms bred in spoilt manna
When the tent shook and Bizarro stole in. "Peace, stranger!"
He wore a chain whereupon the words *No one* had been forged in fire
By alabaster hands. He said, "Henceforth shall those who gaze at the mount
Forget the Man of Tomorrow™, wounded and healed, unclean and wiped."

Lois lifted her veil to draw nigh; the soles of her feet wiped
Holy ground. "Hear my voice," she cried. "Kal-El™ – the alien, sent into the desert
One weeping wailing hour in a snare by that brutish, heart-hardened Luthor™, lying in wait to mount
An assault upon the people of manna –
In captivity, heard the voice of living fire
From the midst of the bush that was not burnt, and became a stranger

Sojourning among us. No other stranger
Hewed stone tablets on which the finger of God wrote, but then wiped
Away those laws while the camp worshipped the calf of gold moulded with fire."
Bizarro clasped her. "Wrath doth wax cold in the desert."
"Yea, I can no longer bear to stomach yesterday's manna,"
Moaned Jimmy, his churning bowels longing for fullness from the mount.

Yea, Lois spake forth, although no one gave her ear. And lo the mount
Shone yellow with the sun going down. "Nothing tastes stranger
Than the bitterness of my soul," mused Jimmy. "Save for manna
Which needs be sweetened. Peradventure would Mister Mxyzptlk deliver?" – he wiped
One nostril eagerly – "Reviled Kltpzyxm would only desert
Us on Earth-2 to make merry." Quiet at first, flames of fire

Descended upon the mount. They smelled of brimstone fire,
The stink of spoilt manna. Kal-El™ cowered and wiped
His tears: the stranger must stay when his people leave the desert.

plod
up teal sod.
  In a mushroom, one peacock-blue Smurf™
  occupies his home turf;
    concealing and flaunting himself like

an
eyespot fan.
  That magician who stalks *Les Schtroumpfs*™
  from those woods, summons nymphs
    just for some love potions from his

pot,
spilt like plot
  twists. Gargamel™ with poisonous self-
  love succumbs to some elf.
    "I'll get you," intimidating

the
taupe villa
  De Smurfen™. So Peyo draws a wife
  from the comics through cartoon life
    of the cels; thereupon artists

link
oil paints, ink-
  outlined *Smurfs' Adventures*™ with sound ef-
  fects synched with Prokofiev
    music, timing each frame-by-frame.

All
whimsical
  names like Smurfette™ make up a motif
  dialect, "smurfing grief,"
    all "smurfy," "smurfish," "smurfiest"

merch-
andised smirch
  called Smurf-A-Getti™, Smurf Berry Crunch™ – cough –
  ice shows, theme parks, spinoff
    PVC figurines dipped in

lead.
Condemned
  alchemy has sold *The Smurfs*™ to spoof
  how licences childproof
    the young. Those culprits age you.

CRUDE SCOOBY™

"Rooby-Rooby-Roo" an accent smacks –
  For cels of cartoon humour from the gumshoe crew;
    For burglars all in costume upon a picture tube;
Van breakdown; meddling kids; ghastly masks;
  Animated and looped – light, layout and glue;
    And áll tráps, the contraptions of Rube.

All choice lingo like "jinkies," like "zoinks, dude";
  "Mysteries are scary, Scooby™! (Where are you?)"
    So lose, find; loose, bind; beshadow, show;
The Greatest Dane whose stress patterns are crude:
                    "Ruh-roh."

ROBOT WORK

Xanadu's mountain tyrant
tycoon now shies from gossip columnists for his press;
his spoils now waste away in piles.
His bird's a singer. His readers
inquired into that other woman;
he's in his bastion.

Jealous of
the visionary freedom
in Samuel Taylor Coleridge's opium,
he burns every
last missive composed in love,
and bars entry.

When credits roll –
you'll hear from the Mercury Theatre,
those voices known from RKO
Radio™. The star baritone
has broadcast through black-and-white jowls.
The stage light cast through the trap door.

But here yours truly
will swear by glasses of Paul Masson® wine;
tongue queued by Pinot Noir cheer,
I hit my mark on the line.
After hiding behind my beard
I've grown unruly.

For an hour
I sit opposite Merv Griffin
to talk Houdini. Quiet on set,
we chew scenery, chinwag chin,
while my cravat steeps in my sweat. . . .
Your cold shower.

The surround sound growls,
"Destiny. You cannot destroy my destiny . . ." I won
the news-flash war of the Martian swarm,
as though my breath had done foley. . . .
I the self transform
into no one –

toy robot, which tricks
something-or-other to do his will.
He menaces some other shill:
black lined, cartoon thing's cheeks puff
about some crystal or stiff stuff
they called the Leadership Matrix.

I thank Hasbro™
for funds to finish my next feature –
an exiled director returns to Hollywood shopping a script.
He shoots his picture short on dough
for payroll, when the film rights are stripped
from an auteur.

THE SCROOGE

That crotchety McDuck is wont to scrooge
His confidence from nephews, or fortune,
And if he chooses the first, seeks refuge
In thoughts of riches, diving into coin.
Once *DuckTales*© have all ended, who's to judge?
Squeeze each penny or drop Dime Number One:
"Bah! Humbug!" comfort of a private vault,
Or daily indulgence, nightly insult.

A TITLE BILLING

Gorging and gorging its tail-hungry core,
The serpent here refers to Steve Gerber.
Man-Thing™ burns fear; at his touch cowards die!
Omega the Unknown™ bursts from the sky;
This gut-split laugh is burst, so near and far
That fraternity of ignorance is scorned;
This jack@$$ takes all credit, while that hack
@$$hat is given full acknowledgement.

Truly some royalty cheque is past due;
Truly a Title Billing is past due.
A Title Billing! Scarcely take those words in,
Then an absurd soul out of Camus's *L'Étranger*
Denies our Lord: from the Ben Day–dotted Everglades
Someone who walks like and swims like and quacks like a duck,
A deadpan gape and witless as a pun,
Is flaunting his bare legs, all the while he
Finds himself "trapped in a world he never made."
Ruffling every feather; how much we owe
The candidate of the All-Night Party
Who hoaxed hairless apes with his voting canard,
For that coarse fowl, billed in the leading role,
Plunges under Hollywood to be sold.

MY AFTER SCHOOL HAIKUS

1. ⇨
- ○ New from ABC,
- ○ Watch CBS for
- ○ Now on NBC,
- ○ PBS presents

2.
- ○ a show for the whole family,
- ○ novelist Francine Pascal's
- ○ the Emmy®-nominated
- ○ a tale based on true events,

3.
- ○ "My Life as a God"
- ○ "After All is Said . . ."
- ○ "The School of Heart Blocks"
- ○ "How Could You Say That?"

4. ⇩
- ○ Lead Jodie Foster
- ○ Fresh-faced Kirk Cameron
- ○ Young Cheryl Arutt
- ○ Heartthrob Scott Baio

12.
- ○ Brought to you by Mars®
- ○ Sponsored by Clairol®
- ○ All thanks to New! Coke®
- ○ From General Foods®

5.
- ○ plays Joe, a gifted flautist,
- ○ stars as hooded-cloak dork, Lou,
- ○ plays Sam, a nervous gymnast,
- ○ stars as fanny-pack brat, Pat,

```
             HMASHMASHMASHMASHMASHMASHMASHM
        ASHMASH              MASHMASHMASHMAS
       MASHM                   SHMASHMASHMASH
       MA      SHMASHMA         MASHMASHMASH
            MASHMASHMASH        ASHMASHMASH
         ASHMASHMASHMASHMA       SHMASHMASH
         HMASHMAS      ASHMAS     HMASHMASH
        SHMASH    MASH  SHMAS     HMASHMASH
        ASHMAS   SHMA HM  HMAS    HMASHMASH
        MASHMAS   SHM HM  HMAS    HMASHMASH
        MASHMAS   SHMA  SHMA      SHMASHMASH
        MASHMASH  HMASHMASHM     ASHMASHMASH
        MASHMASHM  ASHMAS      HMASHMASHMASH
        MASHMASHMAS            ASHMASHMASHMASH
        ASHMASHMASHMASHMASHMASHMASHMASHMASH
         SHMASHMASHMASHMASHMASHMASHMASHMAS
         HMASHMASHMASHMASHMASHMASHMASHM
          MASHMASHMASHMASHMASHMASHMASHMAS
        M      SHMASHMASHMASHMASHM         H
       MAS      MASHMASHMASHMASHMAS       ASH
```

6.
- ○ who made regionals.
- ○ who just got high score.
- ○ who earned top honours.
- ○ who took home the prize.

11.
- ○ because you'll want to know more!
- ○ for it'll be a feel-good hour!
- ○ because you'll need loved ones close!
- ○ for it'll teach a real lesson!

10.
- ○ Don't miss out on this
- ○ Watch this with your kids
- ○ Hurry home to see
- ○ This one is special

- ○ put it in peril.
- ○ turn it all around.
- ○ threaten everything.
- ○ lead to a surprise.

- ○ and an Antarctic plane crash
- ○ as the ozone hole grows could
- ○ and long lines for gas rations
- ○ while the killer bees swarm could

7.
- ○ Still, a pill problem
- ○ But poisoned bonbons
- ○ Only, the wrong crowd
- ○ But dust allergies

⇧   **9.**   **8.**   ⇦

THE CHURCH OF ARCHIE

They gazed into his freckles
 On nose and cheeks sallow,
Between steely eyes hollow,
 With bubbling thoughts shallow,
Still when put inside speech balloons
 His mouth had said instead
An evangelical kiss-off
 From that head of red.

The Spire Christian Comics, daring and dull,
 No shade of grey, no sense of irony,
Nothing too blunt and never too subtle,
 Quite motivated by sanctimony,
 Licensed the characters from The Archies®
And published titles for young born-agains
Without suspicion, lacking any sense.

Out from a van the man without a name
 Showed with scripture verses he was divine
With voice as low and humble as a lamb:
 Never too sharp, said nothing too benign,
 Panel by panel in *Archie's Sonshine*,
He loafed in cut-off jeans on sandy beach
And brought clichés – is this canon? – to preach.

They gazed into his freckles
  At fundamental sorrow,
And quivering with raised hackles,
  Confusion and annoyance,
Still when put inside speech balloons
  Where the humour should have been,
They heard in his sermonizing tone
  Their needs were obscene.

Archie's Date Book exposed the bordello
  Where bold citizens laid (a few cracked wise)
And played the role of john or gigolo;
  A crowd of believers under disguise
  Launched a protest to censure and chastise.
Up to that day Riverdale had ignored
Immoral acts that offended the Lord.

The ignorance of those agnostics, all
  That angst and arrogance about dogma;
Jerry and Debbie had to take a fall,
  They left the faith because of its stigma,
  So their crashing car was no enigma:
Archie's Clean Slate showed what goes after pride,
Those two repented for they almost died.

They gazed into his freckles
  At the love triangle
Of two lasses and one lad
  Turned to such a square,
Flirt, flirt, convert,
  Still when put in a bubble
The good word sounds ambiguous
  As a sham gospel.

The feeble beatnik, living off the dole,
  Enrolled in Riverdale High; called Legion,
He lost control to sex, drugs, rock and roll
  And black magic, which caught like contagion,
  But God found him and he got religion,
No spell or pharmaceutical speeds the pulse
Like turning pages of *Archie's Something Else!*

Both thin-skinned miracles,
  Betty with hair of blonde,
And Veronica wearing black hair,
  Out of pity bawled
At what Christ Jesus taught
  To inspire their shared crush,
The no-good goody-goody Archibald
  So he would live for church.

Upon confessing we seldom made right,
Good ole preachers: we all took for granted
Your humane devotion. Oh, look away
When nobodies are starving while handling the pan when only thumbing out of spite.
Oh, as housewives are fervently, religiously clumping
On their garish mascara, doubtless there will be
Husbands who swear to never let this happen again, thumping
The Gideons beside their motel bed. We seldom regret
An *Enquirer*® story that our ministry taints.
In the wooden cabinet, on a Philips® set,
You sinners are told go and sin no more, but we televised saints
Drop repentant pants to tickle our fancies.

Take Jimmy Swaggart, for example. Oh, the truly
religious
Tuned into his Sunday service; a layman just
Might watch that sob, that moaning distress,
And decide his apology did not look real; an image
As it were of two plump jowls appearing to sponge
up drops of sea
Salt, but some Nielsen® families just refuse to see
Anything special, one man falling for his mistress,
Left nowhere to go to with such soiled baggage.

LADY AND AN ELDER

Father 2bold dropped in
On me one time.
He cried, How can u
Just stand there while I cry?

He cried, I am here 2 tell u
Something, girl.
Have u ever
Heard o' the after world?

I cried, Brother,
If you can't tell
I've long tuned out
The gospel.

He cried, Do u want
2 b led?
I cried, There's feedback
In my head.

He cried, Honey
Let me guide u.
I cried, Sounds like it's
Stuck in a groove!

He cried, I am
Ur messiah
Because I would die
4 u, yeah.
Yeah, I will
Come again.
C ya!

I don't know what he said,
It's been a while,
But, oh, Fr. 2bold
Stayed awhile –
Yeah, I knew who he was
All bible-style.

ODE TO MADONNA

You have guided us, Madonna,
on music videos or commercials,
more fishnet, lace and chiffon
than tunics, sleeves and veils,

less the shine from your manacle rosary,
than your raven-black iron cross,
sacrilegious, yet sorry,
honest, yet ironic.

In a strapless gown with diamonds,
living like all blonde icons of material,
peroxide locks bouncing around –
retail kind of hysteria.

Or a gold corset and a cone bra
atop a cake, as a travesty
of matrimony with a concubine,
only performing virginity.

Mezzo-soprano, F♯
to Middle B, brazen range of an octave
and a half – so who would harp
on lyrics rhyming *of* with *glove*?

Could you conceive how rehearsal
is terminated by the premiere recital?
Could you, in a role reversal,
recite *live* rather than *evil*?

Could we imitate Madonna?
Mouth our vows, knife our palms, lift cans of Pepsi®
while marketing each scandalous fad
from New York dance floors like she?

COUPLET CATCHER

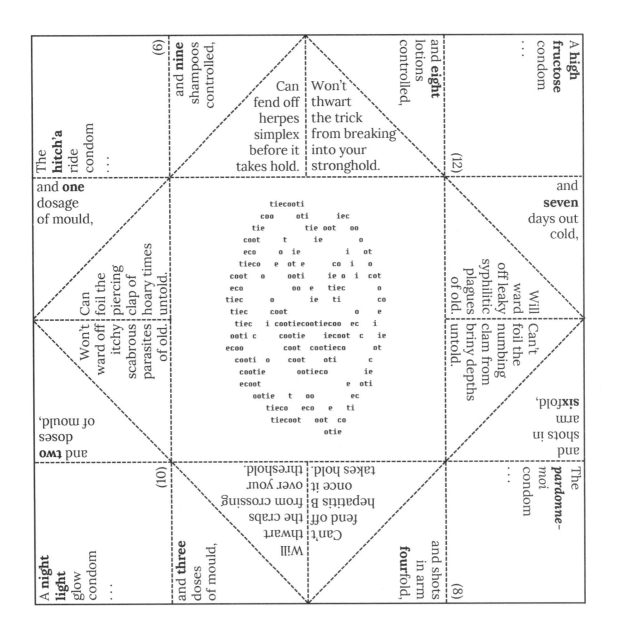

A **high fructose** condom …

and **eight** lotions controlled,

(12)

(6)

and **nine** shampoos controlled,

The **hitch'a** ride condom …

Can fend off herpes simplex before it takes hold. | Won't thwart the trick from breaking into your stronghold.

and **one** dosage of mould,

and **seven** days out cold,

Won't ward off the itchy scabrous clap of parasites of old. | Can foil the piercing hoary times untold.

Will ward off leaky syphilitic plagues of old. | Can't foil the numbing clam from briny depths untold.

and **two** doses of mould,

The **pardonne-**moi condom …

and shots in arm **sixfold**,

A **night light** glow condom …

and **three** doses of mould,

(10)

(8)

and shots in arm **fourfold**,

Will thwart the crabs from crossing over your threshold. | Can't fend off hepatitis B once it takes hold.

COUNTDOWN TO WATCHING *THUNDERBIRDS*™

XIII

Upon remote Tracy Island,
The only resting things
Were torsos of Thunderbirds™.

XII

I got on thin nerves,
Like the wires
On which there hung Thunderbirds™.

XI

Thunderbirds™ filmed in 35 mm.
It was all Supermarionation©.

X

Father and adult sons
Are F.A.B.
Father and adult sons and Thunderbird 1™
Are F.A.B.

IX

I found myself in the middle;
The suspense of SFX
Or the suspense of espionage,
Thunderbird 2™ launching
Or caricature.

VIII

Criminals filled their monitor
With inhumane acts.
The mission of Thunderbirds™:
United to save life.
The Brains
Scrambled the mission
Of International Rescue.

VII

O hoodlums of The Hood,
Why do you enchant family Tracy?
Do you not grasp how Thunderbirds™
Have the upper hand
On the master above you?

VI

Mid-Atlantic accents
And mouthy, tongue-in-cheeky dialogue;
The middle class
Who watched *Thunderbirds*™ enjoyed
Their humour dull.

V

When Thunderbird 3™ lifted off,
It looked modelled
After a Russian shuttle.

IV

In the water Thunderbird 4™,
Swimming in one-third scale,
Looks way out of perspective
From wide angles.

III

Lady Penelope drove Europe
In a pink car.
One time, in disguise,
She sang to deter
Planes flying a mission against
Thunderbirds™.

II

Thunderbird 5™ is orbiting.
Cosmos must be resting.

I

It was first-run syndication.
It was showing
Thunderbirds™ are go!
The puppets swung
In uncharted lands.

THE EVENING CHANT OF A LOST LAND

By outdoor skill we – Marshall, Will
  And Holly – set up camp.
In scales of teal the Sleestak steal
  Around those caverns damp:
Their warning-hiss, a hunt amiss,
  With tail, with claw, with tools.
We campers call: *"Make friends of all*
  Who grok unnatural rules!"

Never outdone, we Marshalls run
  To Pylons and conspire;
When father Rick spins crystals quick
  Those reptile men retire.
Down from a tree two *Pakuni*
  Primitives, Ta and Sa,
Clambered to say, *"Me saku ye"*;
  We spared the child Cha-Ka.

Whoa! By the tent! A violent
  Tyrannosaurus rex!
We moved to quit the old thicket,
  And viewed a time vortex;
Betwixt doorways, Enik relays,
  With Altrusian-gland,
Instructions for the dinosaur:
  "Lost land – decamp lost land!"

We felt bereft once father left,
  But chanced upon his kin;
Then Uncle Jack found our course back
  Along the blonde mountain.
A banjo strums when evening comes,
  And we chant much like fools
From Camp Marshall: *"Make friends of all*
  Who grok unnatural rules!"

A VINCENTINE: TO HIM WHOSE NAME HAUNTS THE FOLLOWING LINES

Venerate him with verse, whose ominous name,
  Mildly reminiscent of Edgar Allan Poe's,
Conjures the baritone that brought him fame
  Onscreen by echoing those slender shadows.
Shiver at every note – what frisson
  Uncanny – an incantation – enchantment
Resonating. What timbre at every tone –
  Those syllables – those beats! A commandment
For no mere mortal could rap above the "Thriller"!
  So do this zombie squeeze, but not that "Monster Mash,"
Because no one wants to dress up in Hallowe'en filler
  When one is wearing pinstriped suits and pencilled 'stache.
In guest appearances on late night TV
  A warm demeanour demonstrated camp as smarmy charm
With snarling lip and brow arching up – quite scary
  But not enough to truly threaten harm.
And were you now to give into the trance
  Like the dour announcer in Castle Frightenstein
Or the despondent inventor of Edward Scissorhands
  You could raise up your junior ghoul by meting out slant rhymes.

AIRING AT NIGHT

1

Courage stuck when the spotlight struck,
When the live audience lost its $#!+,
When the cameraman blew me a kiss;
My stand-up routine took the π!$$,
So I won the crowd with rehearsed wit,
Playing the part of a cocky [=¢{.

2

Network affiliates called it quits:
Stop that smarty-pants, that stupid ¢=~+;
The purse of his lips, his mock pucker,
The arched brow of that ¢*¢{$=¢{&√;
His shrugs more smug, while pulling that stunt,
Than a hustler dealing tats for +!+$.

PAYING AT MORNING

The FCC fined a comedian
For every televised ≈*+#&√[=¢{&√;
A censor or some other mucker
Paid no mind to the words of George Carlin.

EXPLETYPOGRAPHY

$$Q = \% \quad W = \neq \quad E = \& \quad R = \sqrt{} \quad T = + \quad Y = ? \quad U = = \quad I = ! \quad O = * \quad P = \pi$$

$$A = @ \quad S = \$ \quad D = \Delta \quad F = [\quad G = > \quad H = \# \quad J = \text{¿} \quad K = \{ \quad L = <$$

$$Z = \Omega \quad X = \times \quad C = \text{¢} \quad V = / \quad B = \infty \quad N = \sim \quad M = \approx$$

MAD LIBERICKS: JINGLES

Drop Alka-Seltzer® in a _____ of water
<small>NOUN, 1 SYLLABLE</small>

When _____ gives your stomach a spot of bother.
<small>NOUN, 1 SYLLABLE</small>

Whoa! Such digestive grief!

So? Just dissolve relief!

Oh! Plop plop! Oh! Fizz fizz! Those sounds of wonder.

No single gum doubles your investment

In singular pepper _____ refreshment
<small>NOUN, 1 SYLLABLE</small>

Like Double_____® flavour
<small>NOUN, REPEAT PREVIOUS</small>

And scent you must savour

No one duplicates that accomplishment!

Of course you know who named _____ at first sight?
<small>NOUN, 2 SYLLABLES</small>

No? Oscar Mayer® showed us just how to write

It goes B-O-L-O-

Any _____ must know!
<small>PROPER NOUN, 1 SYLLABLE</small>

No? Spell G-N-A 'cause N-E-Y's not right!

From the flag this race _____ me too far.
<small>VERB, 1 SYLLABLE</small>

In this lane the speed _____ me apart.
VERB, 1 SYLLABLE

Gotta take me a break!

Wontcha gimme a _____?
RHYME FOR BREAK, 1 SYLLABLE

My pit stop is a pieca that KitKat® bar!

I don't wanna grow up, just don't wanna grow

'Cause I don't wanna slow down, just don't wanna slow.

_____ will never get rid
ABSTRACT NOUN, 1 SYLLABLE

Of this _____ "R" Us® kid.
CONCRETE NOUN, 1 SYLLABLE

I don't wanna go on, so just lemme go.

from AN ERA FOR ADVERTISING

You must bill me a brand, the best bald-faced symbol
Of old Boyardee® dressing down young Doughboy
For his raw rolls and his burned rubbers,
Nunc est bibendum, the Michelin© Man.

He brewed every bean and each red burro
In his braying country, kicked his cold turkey,
Swilled his Juan Valdez®, saddled his sores
And filtered his flavour, the Marlboro® Man.

From his sneer at the south to the sun up his drawl
Through the brick walls he soldiered, then dissolved powder
Like the washtub preacher who wails, "Oh Yeaahh!"™
A couple quarts per packet, the Kool-Aid© Man.

Back in his day his brain inflated
Some known jazz note, some puzzle notion;
Since "It's Mac Tonight"™, he mocked up a pizza
From rumour and rhyme, a Moonie Man.

Once the tip of his tongue laps up Pop Rocks®,
His stomach cannot keep down Diet Coke®;
Too late for "Mikey, he likes it!"™ who lost his Life®
By the quoted oath, a Quaker® Oats Man.

Check out merchandise with the cashier who punched
The Suggested Retail Price, an accessory
For size-small laymen; so swear off vices
For the motor moustache of the Micro Machines® Man.

Top of Tupperware® tub burps
Call to me, Cellophane me:
Verbal Velcro®, Lego® verbs all;
Your Walkman hum, our mall Muzak.

Buff up Plexi-®, Fiberglas®
Styrofoam™ smooth, AstroTurf® rough.
Grey Frisbees® gyrate Freon™;
Linoleum: limp trampoline.

Plain Aspirin: Adrenalin.
Kleenex® catches my nose Clorox®,
Toxic snot, not Plasticine,
Xerox® toner or Wite-Out®.

We ache, we act. Band-Aid®.
Where's the beef? When we buffet
Zambonis® ooze Vaseline®
Like split Zippers®: zippers spilled.

THE TASTE OF SLIME

The Ph.D.s charged positron colliders
After slamming the receiver. Busting
A Class Five Fully Roaming Vapour proved worse
Than grading undergrads, though. "Disgusting
Blob," Dr. Stantz™ goggled it gulp room service.
Seemingly spooked, it spewed goop. Combusting
Beams chased it off. "Ugh," Dr. Venkman™ swung
Around as slime hit him – even his tongue.

The Minute Maid® execs who saw that on screen
Wanted pitches about the taste of slime.
"Onion," an intern spat out – crickets – "ice cream?"
He packed his desk. "The answer must be lime:
It's green!" A VP swallowed hard. "Wrong. Hi-C®
Is orange. Tangerine, I mean." "But that rhyme:
Try lemon-slime!" "Just add Blue #1
To Citrus Cooler™. Ectoplasm, done."

Twenty-four grams of high fructose corn syrup
Filled each six-ounce Ecto Cooler™ serving.
"I'm Slimer™," one kid burped. A second stirred up
A box to spray fruit juice from the curving
Straw. "Now you're Venkman™," a third kid roared. "Word up!"
They wrote lines since grown-ups were observing.
One slimed kid smirked, "You guys also feel funky?"
"At least we drank our daily vitamin C."

ALTHOUGH SHE WOULD NOT CRUSH THE HORDE

Although she would not crush the Horde™ –
It rudely crushed her soul –
In prison held just for suspense –
Then cut to commercial.

King Hordak™ snarled – he knew nothing
And put down Adora™ –
So for the honour of Grayskull®,
She turned into She-Ra™ –

She raged at Catra™, Captain of Force –
To promote the toy line –
She raged against the Fright Zone™ base –
She raged against Horde Prime™ –

Or rather – it raged on.
He-Man™ entered to rescue her –
'Cause Princess wielded the wrong sword –
Of Protection, not Power –

Now pause to watch advertisements
For Mattel® merchandise –
She-Ra™ was cast as He-Man's™ twin
From pastel paradise.

Each episode repeats the plot –
'Til kids finally catch on
And buy into those plastic thoughts
They see in syndication.

a lot figures
into

the grey Trans-
former™

glued to thin
cardboard

within a clear
blister.

That radiation from debris over miles:
Sale racks in a lit, slick aisle.

RUXPIN™

The cassette in your back
Should speak to adolescents;
Still I turned down the soundtrack:
As playing made me tense.

I read before the inks
Rubbed off those picture books;
Your servomotored blinks
Would flash me scowling looks.

Your snout mouthing each line
Was powered by *C* batteries;
When tapes ran short on time
Your nostrils squealed and wheezed.

I tore apart your seams
With looped screeching in my ears,
You played me off to dreams
Of moribund plush bears.

A HOOT

It is day in the neighbourhood is a beautiful day for a neighbour is a neighbourly day in this beauty wood. But Mr. Rogers felt alone. He felt tight as a buckled belt and tied tie.

But could you be what you seem, could you be a bellow could you be howl could you be horn or could you be a stage whisper could you be a steam whistle could it be beak, beak from the sky oh my you are a hoot, a hoot when a neighbour. But you escaped from an eggshell in a nest but you were only make-believe to Mr. Rogers but you were as lonely as one could be for you were once in an eggshell for no one knows loneliness as an owl alone in an eggshell but you were only make-believe for you made feathers blue not grey you made eyes white not grey so Mr. Rogers eased through sleeves of his cardigan.

So he started to croon.

A friend escaped from an eggshell
Owl owl.
A friend escaped from an eggshell
So well oh well.
Owl owl.
His name is X, short for Escape, his name is X for he escaped, so I escape along with X owl
owl from an eggshell.
Owl owl owl
Owl owl.
You croon along oh so well.

So they crooned oh well oh well oh well for they laughed for laughter's sake oh well for they escaped through make-believe believe believe.

OH! PORTMANTEAUS!

Oh, portmanteaus! Lonely Once-ler,
Whose factories knitted the Thneeds,
Felled those forests where Bar-ba-loots were,
While euphemisms damped down his deeds.

While machines discharge Shloppity Shlop,
One moustached Lorax opposed Once-ler,
Dampening each sound of axe chop,
As though Truffula trees cannot hear.

JABBERJAWKY

Ain't bousing you, that rhythy wyrm
  Could jive, but jangled on the noives:
Real nasey was his tungaskirm,
  But the Neptunes got moives.

"Respect! Hey, Jabberjaw™, why peck
  At fills, or whack out riffs? Go thwack
Backbeats as Hihats clash! Go wreck
  That krupious Snaredrumcrack!"

He gripped two welker sticks in fins;
  In time the poifect tone he struck
When walloped he on those Tomtom skins
  A breakdown with dumb luck.

So, avish fans clamoured to face
  The Jabberjaw™ with gills so chill
Just kicking on that rumbey Bass
  With new wave on the bill!

Da-*dum*! Da-*dum*! They strummed. He drummed
  Both welker rods with fluid-flow
While singing lead! His vocals freed
  Soiten keys high and low.

"Show some respect! Hey, Jabberjaw™,
  You wailed out there, o nautish fool!"
"Clam right we rocked out! Nyuk, nyuk, nyuk."
  He chuckled from the stool.

Ain't bousing you, that rhythy wyrm
  Could jive, but jangled on the noives:
Real nasey was his tungaskirm,
  But the Neptunes got moives.

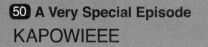

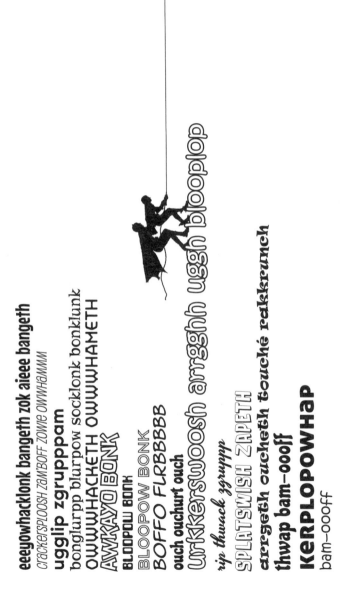

POWER GOES COMMANDO AFTER BOOT-⇧

POWER goes commando after boot-⇧,
⇧-load a *Contra*™ cheat at title screen;
Run, gun unto the ending of shut- ⇩

⇩-low code in one- or two-player mode
I know for puberty forked this ⇦-brained,
⇨-minded gamer to go commando.

Good guys, side-scrolling by, fight from ⇦ to
⇨wrongs of vile Red Falcon aliens.

(Buttons on the Nintendo® controller
are not in alphabetical order.)

Run, gun into eight-direction shoot-⇧.

⇧-scale rifles with limitless ammo,
And race, cruel fate, to conquer the count- ⇩
⇩-grade guerillas going commando.

Bad guys, Sandinista front, ⇦-handed,
⇨-winged forces blaze South Americans.
Run, gun up to eight-bit villains ⇦ and

⇨-on, my programmer, Hiroshita,
Curse, bless me now with thirty lives, to B
A Konami® coder gone commando.
Run, gun upon pressing the button START.

```
Press any key to continue.
PIC4          DAX          91,885 03-06-1988 15:24
PIC5          DAX          46,750 03-06-1988 15:24
PIC6          DAX          66,888 03-06-1988 15:24
PIC7          DAX          67,804 03-06-1988 15:24
PIC8          DAX          67,227 03-06-1988 15:24
POOL          CFG          44     03-06-1988 15:24
RANDCOM       DAX          755    03-06-1988 15:24
SAVGAMA       DAT          13,137 03-06-1988 15:24
SETUP         EXE          25,678 03-06-1988 15:24
```

Toss out twelve-sided dice of past campaigns
At "C:\cd POOLRAD" command string;
Forget the character each sheet contains,
Type "C:\POOLRAD> start.exe STING".

Before the software loads its menu screens,
Type "STING" to stop passwords from computing;
The *Pool of Radiance* program routines
Prompt MS-DOS to start executing.

Minus a Dungeon Master, game menus
Scroll out Dungeons & Dragons® franchising;
They roll the classes, races and values
That our six-man party's exercising.

Although the first-person view disappoints
With the 3-D window of landscaping;
We level up with experience points
While studying clumsy texture mapping.

When Tyranthraxus the possessor mounts
His sneak attack on the port city Phlan,
The display shifts to three-quarter view and counts
Hit points in combat mode simulation.

In spite of how this role-playing game acts
Keystrokes cannot stop humans competing;
They swap the wisdom of Gary Gygax
For "C:\POOLRAD>" plain text editing.

```
START       EXE        47,936 03-06-1988 15:24
START       EX_        47,936 03-06-1988 15:24
TITLE       DAX        33,898 03-06-1988 15:24

Press any key to continue.
WILDCOM  DAX            5,786 03-06-1988 15:24

   137 File(s)        1,656,603 Bytes.
     1 Dir(s)

C:\POOLRAD>
```

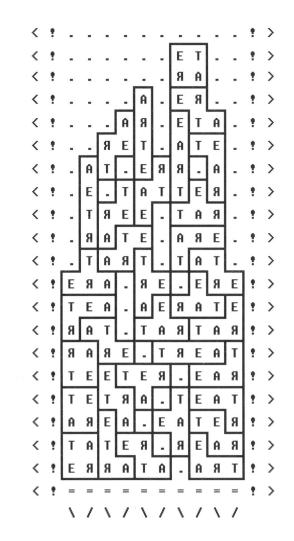

```
        lda flowerState
        and #F$F0
        cmp #FLOWER_REVIVED | (1 * 16)
        bne .doneEasterEggCheck
        bit easterEggStatus
        bmi .doneEasterEggCheck
        lda collectedCandyPieces
        cmp #7
        bne .setEasterEggStepNotDone
        lda easterEggStatus
        and #3
        cmp #3
        bne .checkIfETTookPhonePiece
        lda #2
.checkIfETTookPhonePiece
        tax
        lda phonePieceAttributes,x

        bpl .setEasterEggStepNotDone
        ldx easterEggStatus
        cpx #2
        bcs .setEasterEggStepDone
        lda EasterEggSpriteValues,x
        sta easterEggSpriteFlag
        lda #50
        sta currentObjectVertPos
.setEasterEggStepDone
        sec
        bcs .setEasterEggStatusFlags

.setEasterEggStepNotDone
        clc
.setEasterEggStatusFlags
        lda easterEggStatus
        rol
        ora #DONE_EASTER_EGG_CHECK
        sta easterEggStatus
        and #DONE_EASTER_EGG_STEPS
        cmp #DONE_EASTER_EGG_STEPS
        bne .doneEasterEggCheck
        lda #SHOW_HSW_INITIALS_VALUE
        sta programmerInitialFlag
.doneEasterEggCheck
        rts
```

Nothing awakens you, E.T.®,
Floating over bitmapped landscape;
You, dimmest sprite of Atari®,
Whose finger glows around Easter eggs.

Howard Scott Warshaw coded keys
For his 128B RAM headache;
Something awakens you, Indy®,
Undertaking eight-bit escapes.

You, bright players with memories
Of thumbs throbbing asleep and awake,
Ask how could anything like this be?
For this 4KB ROM mistake
Trashed all of Silicon Valley.

```
                                       SCORE

                              PN G   IM 0   0
                              QO H   JN 1   1
                                 G  FL•P   F
                                 H  GM•Q   •
                                    FNJ•G3
                                    GOK•H5
Now comes the level when,           P GPK
Each Pac-Man™ game seizes           50Q HQL
This raster spasm of              "H  FGL  00
A software bug or just            "I  GHM  11
                                  "PP  M
The kill-screen labyrinth         "QQ  N
Makes players sacrifice                    0N00   6
A hardware malfunction                     10     A7
Then "Game Over" flickers         PP 0
                                  QQ 1 0
While four enemies chase          B P P02
The PCB runs its                  C0Q Q13
           "2C06 3E04  READY!1J G
Pressing the hormonal             12K H1
                                  "          KPF 0
Our consciousness loops           "          LQ• 1
Some programmer at Namco®          FB LG1 ⊚   7
Controlling the joystick             •C MH2 P   8
With phantom memories              N M P3 0
                                   0 N Q5 1
                                   I N0G
                                   J 01H
                                  FB            B
                                  GC          C
                                  DB    NNN 05
                                  EC    000 17
```

HIGH

●●

```
...........
 .      .
●       .
 .      .
...........
 .      .
 .      .
......  ...
        .

 .
 .
 .
 .

 .
 .
 .
 .

 .
...........
 .   .   .
 .   .   .
●..  ......
  .  .   .
  .  .   .
......  ...
 .      .
 .      .
...........
```

clipping a screen image,
Commodore® processors;
pixels could be either
a defective cartridge!

possesses C64®s
our dot-hungry savage;
or just a design glitch?
one graphic-chip eyesore!

ghastly plots of revenge,
"fruit" subroutine error:
LD A,#04"
start button of teenage . . .

RGB light patterns for
confused C Language;
depression of old age . . .
in microcomputers!

You will know it's time to slobber like Pavlov's Labrador when you hear, "Sit, Ubu, sit."

You will know it's time to spell *poor* – or was that *pore*? or *pour*? – when you hear the Texan drawl of Speak & Spell™.

When you hear "Everybody Wants Something" by the Zit Remedy you will know that earworm turned your skull into the cocoon for its cacophonous pupa.

You will know it's time to "transform this decayed form to Mumm-Ra the Ever-Living" when you hear the incantation – if by "decayed" you mean "scrawny," and by "Mumm-Ra the Ever-Living" you mean "Alpha the Never-Crying."

You will know it's time to turn away when you hear the wink of a teddy bear – which must've been stuffed with a demon legion by Lucifer himself – after the closing credits of *The Many Adventures of Winnie the Pooh*™.

You will know it's time your stomach knots up when you hear D.J. Tanner dial 555-6410 to call her boyfriend – because you wished on every candle you've ever blown out on every birthday cake that your phone would ring.

You will know "it's fun to smoke marijuana" when you hear the backmasking in the chorus of "Another One Bites the Dust" while hotboxing in the downstairs bathroom.

You will know it's time to just go down to Blockbuster® to rent the pan-and-scan tape already when you hear John McClane yell "Yippee-ki-yay, Mr. Falcon!"

You will know it's time to turn down the volume when you hear "Ici Radio-Canada" because it's after midnight and you're about to watch a risqué foreign movie, and you can't let your parents hear.

You will know it's time to turn in when you hear crackling static after "O Canada," which the government should've replaced with Alanis's "Too Hot" years ago.

SCHOOLHOUSE _____!

ACROSS

4 "It's a hot spot, it's a _____!"
   ("Interplanet Janet")
5 "Look at those movin' _____!"
   ("Body Machine")
8 "_____ Room"
9 "Multiply seven times seven,
   Take forty-nine _____ right up to seventh
   heaven."
   ("Lucky Seven Sampson")
11 "And now we pull down on
   the lever, _____ our ballots."
   ("Sufferin' Till Suffrage")
12 "___oter Computer and Mr. Chips
   They've got the answers
   at their fingertips."
   ("Number Cruncher")
15 "Ga_____eo!"
   ("A Victim of Gravity")
16 *SCHOOLHOUSE _____!*
19 "_____ is a Magic Number"
20 "Introducing the greatest
   show on _____"
   ("The Weather")
22 "Milk and honey,
   _____ and butter,
   Peas and rice."
   ("Conjunction Junction")
23 "When I use my imagi__ion
   I think, I plot, I plan,
   I dream."
   ("Verb: That's What's Happening")

DOWN

1 "I took a ferry to the Statue of Liberty.
   My best friend was waiting there for me.
   (He took an _____ ferry.)"
   ("A Noun Is a Person, Place, or Thing")
2 "_____ this or that; grow thin or fat.
   Never mind, I wouldn't do that,
   I'm fat enough now!"
   ("Conjunction Junction")
3 "Oh, I took a train, took a train,
   To another _____."
   ("A Noun Is a Person, Place, or Thing")
6 "Nuclear and thermal and _____,
   If we miss, we'll get colder and colder."
   ("The Energy Blues")
7 "Without Earth's gravity
   To keep us in our place,
   We'd have no weight at all,
   We'd be in outer _____."
   ("A Victim of Gravity")
10 "When you run out of digits,
   You can _____ all over again."
   ("My Hero, Zero")
13 "Mother Edison worked late each _____,
   It went well until the fading light."
   ("Mother Necessity")
14 "But I wonder who that sad little _____
   of paper is?" ("I'm Just a Bill")
17 "The Shot _____ 'Round the World"
18 "Burnin' fuel
   And usin' _____
   They generate . . ."
   ("Electricity")
21 "Now the blood's not _____,
   It's kinda special,
   Come dig it, Circulation!" ("Do the Circulation")

LOUSES _____HOOCH!

SOLUTIONS

```
  E       E   S
G A S   P A R T S
  R       S   T A S
E L B O W   S T E P S
  Y       L   S E   A
        C A S T     S C O
  N   R     A   S E
L I L     R O C K
  G     H   T   R S
T H R E E   E A R T H
  T     A   B   P E
      B R E A D   N A T
      D     D       M
```

```
          C   I       T   A
          O R A L S   T H I N G
  T       A   L   H E   T
T A R P S   B E A R D
  R   S     S   A E   P
A T E       C O R K   D A B
  S   M     A   T H   C
          P E S T S   L A Y E R
  S   A         C   R S
T A S T E   B O W E L
  G   S         S   D
```

Warning regarding *Care Bears*™: Immature
  Audiences may misunderstand
That fabricated and miniature
  Animals have a magic gland.

Watching an animated bear
  That cares has taught many
About co-operative "stares"
  Calming bad company.

As caring bear watchers
  Have navel-gazed,
An angry amateur's
  Beating has dazed.

Message
A villain imagines a bare stomach
  Attracts an abusive attack.

BOB BROADCASTS BANKRUPT BEAUTY BOOB BY BOOB

Bob's broadcast objectifies buxom blondes
By branding labourers "Barker's Beauties,"
But beauties believe labels out-of-bounds
Because Bob barters labouring booties,
Balancing bums beside subjugation.
Rebellious beauties lob public bombshells,
Battling about dumb masturbation,
But Barker dive-bombs libellous rebels.
Subject broached, CBS boys reimbursed Bob.
Broadcasters back bankable behaviour,
But banished beauties above Barker's job,
Thereby brand-new "Barker's Beauties" labour.
Bob broadcasts bankrupt beauty boob by boob
But beauties abide beyond brand-name tube.

PROTOCOL

Concerning social protocol,
courtesy, tact, patience,
C-3PO™ comes across cold.

Panic attacks
short-circuit sentience.
Cognition circuitry lacks

coping mechanisms
which process melancholy –
hence criticisms

breaching common decency.
C-3PO™ ironically
respects privacy

because electronic voices echo.
Controlling secrets excites C-3PO™.

DROIDS™

Stupid astro-droid, stunted tripod, oldest friend:
radar displays dim, vocoder devices fade,
hard drives grind . . . indeed, degradation
draws doomed droids toward dubious episodes –
abandoned behind shields amid bombardments,
kidnapped outside barricades during raids,
dented lightspeeding around asteroid fields
and dismembered landspeeding down sand dunes.
Should Darth Vader™ jeopardize diplomacy,
Jedi™ would demand immediate surrender,
and droids could discourse, read, decipher . . .
Domed sidekick, droll and madcap confidante,
letter-digit–letter-digit, R2-D2™,
codes adventure inside gelded, golden disks.

Hearing the weekly secret lets me scream,
Releasing pressure gathered over years
Kept after class. The grade five self-esteem
Rarely survives those prepubescent peers.
Each episode begins when Pee-wee™ shares
The secret utterance. He tells viewers,
"Please scream whenever friends speak unawares.
Let them believe they accidentally cursed."
Enacting Pee-wee™ stories gets attention
Between grey classes where we rehearse
Boredom before they make me serve detention
Since classmates heard me accidentally curse.
When teachers hear me emcee they are peeved
Because they never get the stories he weaved.

SNARF™

Planetfall of fauna, flora, fungi:
Fire, after warfare, safari spacecraft
Fled, flew off, fuelled from suffering, grief.
Few feline refugees formed families,
Figurative force fields. Fantasy elf (dwarf?)
Furry-, frisky-, fuzzy-, fraidy-cat Snarf™
Forages food off floors of forest fierce,
Finds fruit from ferocious foliage.
Snarf™ feeds kinfolk. Chief, fighters, followers
Forfeit further safety defending life,
Defeating shape-shifting, mummified fiends.
Often afraid, Snarf™ offers, "Snarf, snarf,"
Signifying, "Fend off foul, awful feelings.
Friends, cat fight for freedom forever!"

THROUGH GOLDEN AGES GIRLS LODGE TOGETHER

Through golden ages girls lodge together;
  Through generations girls encourage laughs.
Naughty young Georgian urges gals gather,
  Mingle, gossip, manage long paragraphs;
Gentle Norwegian daughter neglects thought,
  Gleefully living during teasing rough;
Rigid governess begrudges getting caught
  Gambling, feigns dignity acting tough;
Fragile *ragazza* migrant indulges strange
  Magic, reigns vigorously being strong.
Geriatric group ignores bogus change,
  Sings unforgettably nostalgic song:
Thoroughly grateful partygoers forgo
Giving big gifts, betraying largest ego.

HULK HOGAN'S 24" PYTHONS

Whoever hears the whispers through his moustache
should change their behaviour. Both pythons
have smothered other heels whenever they match:
his whiskers hiss, his headlock tightens,

his champions cheer. These Hulkamaniacs™
cherish the thought, charisma, physique
behind each stretch, choke, hook, clutch, hold, chop, bash,
which characterizes well-honed technique.

The Sheik™ held hostage the championship
with cheapest shots rather than honest throws
while threatening those authentic heroes;

The Hulkster™ shook that heavyweight cheat,
finishing their skirmish with the Irish Whip.
Brother, ethics shape this champion athlete!

Nothing in silver mist, like nothing which
　Hides everything in mysterious bright,
　Avoids infrared detection tonight
Since Michael Knight™ flicked his night-vision switch,
　Investigating behind crimson light:
　Knight Industries built this Firebird with sight;
Its vehicle gained hi-tech consciousness futuristic
　With insight into criminals outright!
I emulate chivalry via this circuit,
　I activate bits amid memories,
　I activate chips amid inquiries,
　Encoding via this microprocessor;
Consider illogical logic within KITT™! –
　I, knight, alongside Michael Knight™, rider.

MAJESTY

Jordan enjoyed jamming
Jumpshots, jumpers, js.
Rejoice, M.J. joked.
Conjure hallelujahs!

Jealous, Johnson Jr.
Judged Jordan's jabber.
Jeepers, Johnson
Interjected.

Journalists junketed.
Just joking, Jr.
Jeered. Jocular
Jordan cajoled Johnson.

Jr. rejected
M.J.'s majesty.

SPOCK™S SPOKEN-WORD TRACKS

"Hark! Freaky, dark, unmistakable treks,
Rocketing amok like wicked Sputnik!"
Swank Spock™s spoken words market awkward shtick,
Making trademarked gimmicks, banking paycheques;

"Alack, disk jockeys like dreck!" Spock™ kvetches.
"Fake funky racket, hokey rocky clack,
Shrieking, squeaking, squawking background muzak,
Mock-heroic skits, hacky-joke sketches –

"Skilful tracks acknowledge gawky klutzes,
Invoking skilled mind-tricks, neck-pinches – Spock™-like,
Evoking wacky Klingon™ makeup kits.

"Frankly speaking, knowledge takes *Kolinahr:*
Schmucks speak malarkey; keep thinking kosher!"
Keen Spock™ talks remarkable folklore – schlock-like.

MILLI VANILLI

I'll call 1-800-DIAL-MTV®
Pleading, "Look, play wholehearted love ballads
Like 'Girl . . .'" although they'll neglect heartfelt pleas,
Flashing commercials until knuckleheads
Stupidly flip channels. I'll redial, "Please –
Look, cable television lacks all style,
Only publicizing itself, really –
Play 'Girl . . .'" although they'll simply indulge guile,
"Flamboyant lampoon delivers scandal:
'Laud gilded idols, Milli Vanilli,
Popular single, album, ensemble.'
Should listeners replay fraudulent vocals?"
"Vanilla lyrics, millionaire's sample,
Plus lip-flap melodies rule musicals!"

McDonaldland™ welcomes wholesome families. Come home! Mingle among community made from trademarked McDonald's™ merchandise. Human ambassadors promote famous menu items, McChicken™, McNuggets™, McRib™. Man-sized hamburger mascots market economic meal combos. Permanently campaigning, Mayor McCheese® promises all-American meat. Hamburglar®, shameless criminal, mugs many customers…millions! Mischievous Grimace® amuses himself. (Impishly resembling some smirking milkshake? Smug mountain? Simpering pimple?) Become McDonaldland™ members! A.M. means chomping custom-made McMuffins™! P.M. means munching gourmet McPizza™! Perform McDonald's® prime-time anthem: "Twoallbeefpatties specialsaucelettucecheesepicklesonions onasesameseedbun™." Meanwhile, welcoming commercials imply uncomfortable humour. Wholesome families must consume familiar McDonaldland™ members!

SONNET N

Now snack – snack on California Raisins™,
No lunch box nosh around noontime contends
Against nighttime munchies Nature sends
On bunches wrinkled during barren seasons;
Neither print on menus, nor ink on napkins
Incite pangs inside hungry paunches
Sooner than Sun-Maid® in brown-bag lunches,
Shining upon diners between kitchens –

On Motown® singin', moonwalk dancin'
California Raisins™ now snack . . . Claymation®
Advertisement campaigns shrink well-known
RnB musicians into Plasticine®
And manipulate one vintage emotion,
Tenderness! No one dines on wrinkles alone.

COSBY SONNET

Bought – so Jell-O®
broke those round copper moulds
of homes from your childhood;
announcing frozen Pops™
to savour or swallow –
low calories!
Sold – so goes on
spokesman scold Dr. Cosby,
fooling around;
also eight-year-olds
from movie studios
improvise routines,
humouring our Cos
for money, found!

Centipede™ drops points upon top players.
Upright coin-op euphoria per play.
Centipede's pincers spike pulse tempo.
Centipede picks up speed.
Pulse pumps capillaries
Rapidly pounding shoot-'em-up platforms.

Pesticide propels explosions.
Sparks split apart centipede opponents
Parts spread paralyzing poison:
Spiders, caps, scorpions.
Rapturous computer graphics display.
Compulsion pixelates pro players.
Pressure suppresses dopamine.
Fingertips zap pests, taps spray repellent.

ELOQUENCE QUA MYSTIQUE

Q™ requited eloquence qua mystique.
Q™ required quests – queries acquired.
Q™ requested inquiries quite oblique.

Q™ equated quester manqué squired.
Q™ equalled pique frequently picaresque
Prequel q-rated, sequel inquired.

Q™ quit antique, brusque, querulous burlesque
Masquerading mosquito quasi-squished
Baroque banquet, masque, requisite grotesque.

Opaque quotations quietly vanquished;
Squirmy pipsqueak squawked quantum technique,
Quote loquacity unquote relinquished.

Qwerty Quixote quilled tranquil critique;
Q™ requited eloquence qua mystique.

CARTOON BUTTERFLY

Your rainbow streams anywhere.
Are dragons breathing fire? Friends, pretend.
Astronauts observe Earth through their visors.

LeVar reads clear. LeVar
from popular *Roots* or *ReBop* obscure,
LeVar
our bardic actor, for minor viewers
performs stories: scripts roles. (Neither classroom, nor after-school program.)

Armchair scholars observe our universe
from libraries!
LeVar revives fluttery
discovery
or transformative theory.
LeVar trades realism for reverie; generations read,
their spectrum bursts through history.

She styled herself as Chrissy! Yes, Pastor
Snow christened his first-born offspring "Christmas"
Because she was religious, autonomous,
Capitalist – also alabaster
As Santa's loins. Sporting polyester
Plus spandex, Chrissy strikes viewers as famous
Beside those sitcom roommates surely jealous
Since she styled herself using ThighMaster™!
So style yourself opposite star actress
Suzanne Somers! She knows squeezing, squeezing knees
Against spring-loaded resistance builds fitness!
Strengthen legs, shape thighs, shed hips – silly tease!
Yes, style yourself as Chrissy does! Witness
Some fashionable results such as these.

THIS TV SPOT

This TV spot confronts lightweights. "Listen,
Youngsters!" it starts out. "Team with Mr. T™
At breakfast." Then animation lists ten
Activities to create history.
"First, eat these vitamin-fortified oats!
Next, stretch" – but what about those without gifts? –
"After that, sprint, somersault, pivot, float,
Squat, tumble, vault" – about those with doubts? – "lift."
Live-action Mr. T™ enters to point
At those with questions. "Time to get sweating!"
Immature T™ wrestled doubt at gunpoint,
But Mr. trains gifted athletes. Getting
That Mr. T™ beat out adversity
Motivates twerps to defeat self-pity.

PEGASUS

Zeus suffered under Daedalus's rule,
until you summoned Pegasus,
mounting your last-minute
rescue.

Through quaint language you routed
our usurper cruel.
"Plumed equine! Guard Mount Olympus!"
"Uh-oh! Hercules!"

Thunderbolts struck around your knuckle.
Your muscles burst
abundant.

Our ousted ruler cursed.
"Must you bluster thus? Must you tussle?"
"Surely Zeus would return triumphant!"

via VHS, vis-à-vis VCR
review every event, view over JVC®
view over services, review over device
archive video via VHS

view live TV, view over TV services
review vis-à-vis VCR over JVC®
observation never reserved, available forever
addictive delivery view via VHS

save visibly conventional evening movie version
save revolutionary verbal overnight movie version
compulsively leave even-handed videotapes
give videotapes obsessive goings-over

video archive VCR device
review via VHS, view reverse vision

Whom will we worship? With which weekly show?
  Wonder Woman™! When will viewers bow down?
  Wednesdays! Which warrior wins network renown?
Wonder Woman™! Why will viewers bow low?
Wielding weapons – broadsword, arrows, longbow –
  Wonder Woman™ twirls without weighty brawn!
  Weighing wisdom – highbrow, lowbrow, well known –
Wonder Woman™ brawls with unwieldy woe!
While weak followers wrestle unawares
  Wonder Woman™ bestows awesome warnings;
When wary followers weakly withdraw
  Wonder Woman™ wrests woeful, worthless swears;
  Where followers waver between two wrongs
Wonder Woman™ waves away weary law.

*SUPER*BETAMAX®

Index explains Pro-X™ oxide   Mixer
exposes flux multiplexing lux   AUX
coaxial extension box complex

                                       Ex.

execute exact excellence approx.
experts fix external fixtures   extra
super-deluxe pixels   Maximum suffix
Alex, ALEX Excuse expenditure, next   EXT.
exactly extreme exits. exercises.   expanding
homosexual?   exists. six-double-five-three-two-one.
experimental reflex   Excellent.
Alexander expecting sixth experience
paradoxically excitement sex
explain climax,
x1/10 x1/5 x1 x2   Betamax® text

Yes, Gumby®! Pokey®? Yes! Why, Davey®? Touchy clay
Playmates parody your wry personality;
Yes, Gumby®! They say showy mutability
Betrays mysteriously wearying decay.

"My buddy Pokey®?" Yes! "Why?" Your dopey pony
Enjoys yanking easygoing anatomy;
"My preachy buddy?" Yes! "Why, Davey®?" Your chummy
Playmate uneasily eyeballs acrimony.

Why, Gumby®? "My underlying anxiety
Absolutely stymies Toyland™ society
Beyond every stereotypical story;

"Say sorry, Pokey®! Why try clumsy betrayal?
Playmates any hypocritical portrayal
Conveys cynicism. Yes, Davey®! Say sorry."

CANONIZE ZELLERS

Canonize Zellers. Rhapsodize Cheez-Its®,
Cheezies, Cheez Whiz. Characterize Squeezit®s
Lazy, sleazy Ritz, Utz® scuzzy. Emblaze
Zagnut®s stanzas. Orbitz™ blazons amaze.
Romanticize Twizzlers®, nuzzling schnozzes.
Eroticize schmaltzy, muzzled ZotZ®es.
Putzes sentimentalize squeezed Heinz®es;
Yutzes seize commercialized sizes.
Chintzy Ziploc®s allegorize laissez-
Faire. Economized Zoodles® symbolize
Citizenry. Glitzy, sizzling Zippo®s
Monetize Zig-Zag®s. Prized Sleep-eze®s doze.
Soliloquize Zest®. Noxzema® fizzes.
Ventriloquize Pez®. Bazooka® oozes.

NOW YOU KNOW, AND KNOWING MAKES YOU A SUPERSTAR!

COLOUR BY TECHNICOLOR®

You feel lost? Smarten up! Now, think about the place where you feel most at home, even if it's imaginary like Never-Never, Wonder- or even Oompa-Loompa Land. If you don't know the way, ask a local for directions, even if you can't quite remember the lyrics of the song those mischievous indentured labourers sang along the path to the Emerald City. I've got a feeling, my pretty . . . you'll forget Kansas soon enough!

BRIQUETTE

Hey, looks like you're coughing up smoke and/or sloughing burnt skin. You must be *en flambé!* Quick, drop to your hands and knees. Now, fumble around to find the tunnel that leads out of the cave. You probably shouldn't have awoken that most specially greedy, strong and wicked worm. Huh, Bilbo?

SWIMMER'S EAR

Ignore whatever it is that kinda smells like lollipops. Forget whatever it is that sorta looks like a swirling rainbow. That's not Candy Land® - there is an oil spill on the lake! Unless you want to make-believe you're a sticky seagull, take a dip somewhere else. To quote Bob Ross, a painter known for his oils, "Exxon™ doesn't make mistakes, just happy little accidents."

SWEET MAMA ONOMATOPOEIA

It's got to be rough – *ruff!* – to be cast out of pleasant
society. Just look at this here werewolf . . . look at it. Don't
make eye contact! How'll – *howl!* – you know if he's hungry?
Remember, lycanthropes can smell fear and some breeds might even
read thoughts. Don't even think about – *bow-wow!* – red meat!

I ♥ RED MEAT

Before beginning construction, get the blueprints for your
project approved by a board-certified inspector. Anything worth
building is worth planning for. It's procedure! (Sponsored by
the International Brotherhood of Teamsters® – unions built US
strong!)

LIBRETTO

Forget what Briquette told you before. If you're coughing up
smoke and/or sloughing layers of burnt skin, whatever you do,
don't just fumble around! Wrap yourself in a rug, a blanket or
torn rags to smother the flames. Then steal away into an opera
house, cut a mask in half and learn to play the pipe organ,
electric guitar and synthesizer.

BABY FACE KAYFABE

Only a phony SEAL like Torpedo® or one of the other G.I. Joe®
poseurs would ever doggy-paddle in the shallow end of a public
pool – and you're no loser, are you? Tread water in the deep end

(BABY FACE KAYFABE, cont'd)

like a winner! Kick your legs like a backup dancer. Keep up a hip-hop tempo! Cup your hands like you're going to make First Sergeant Duke® taste your righteous backhand! Repeat after me: "You wouldn't know how to rehearse military manoeuveres if they slapped the camo paint off your face!"

SHE-PEER PRESSURE

Even if you're not so sure whether in the right, never turn down a good, clean fight. Why not give bare-knuckle boxing a go? Give fisticuffs a try! No eye gouging, hair pulling or fish hooking, though. And nothing below the belt. Don't get beaten – get even!

STARRING TINA TURNER AS AUNTY ENTITY

Looks like Max Rockatansky ran out of gas for his rig. Clearly he's jinxed. A mutant gang must've paid a witch doctor for a hex. If you want to reverse the curse, cut off the heads of a dozen chickens, string them around your neck with twine, swallow a handful of their tail feathers and roost on a few of their eggs. It'l take you some doing to undo voodoo.

CORPORAL TUNNEL SYNDROME

Whoa, close call! I couldn't see you there! No wonder, you don't have any reflectors on that creaky rickshaw. Reflectors are necessary to let vehicles, never mind those other runners, know where you are. Remember, when you have to haul wealthy Western

(CORPORAL TUNNEL SYNDROME, cont'd)

tourists around Seoul between shifts hunched over a light box
at the animation studio, be sure to have the proper safety
equipment on your cart.

SIREN'S SONG (A.K.A. WOMANATEE)

You'll never learn to water ski while standing on the shore,
landlubber! They don't call it dirt skiing, do they? Never quit!
Ever. Not even when you're swallowing salt water by the mouthful
like some shipwrecked survivor clinging to a lifeboat.

> Yo ho, yo ho, the pirate death!
> Our vessel's taking water
> A hoary tale, you'll tell it best
> From Davy Jones's locker!

PRODUCT ENLARGED TO SHOW TEXTURE

Never tell anyone your name, your age or when you'll be home
alone. Don't give up your privacy so easily! Your dear Father
in Heaven says you must save your precious, sweet, tender . . .
innocence. For marriage. No premarital hanky-panky, missy. True
love waits. Say, isn't that skirt showing a little too much leg?

LADY DOCTOR JEKYLL

How many times do I have to tell you? You can't plan a mistake;
a mistake is what happens when you don't plan. Was it a mistake

(LADY DOCTOR JEKYLL, cont'd)

to concoct a potion and test it on yourself? No! To transform
into a cold-blooded, dead-eyed sociopath? Well, yes. To cook up
a serum to prevent you from turning ever again? See? Even though
it's plan B, it's still a plan.

GRETA

Don't pull the fire alarm unless you're coughing up smoke and/
or sloughing off layers of burnt skin. It isn't a firefighter's
job to put out your pranks. If you've got to pull an alarm like
a proper new-batch Gremlin™, be sure to set something on fire
before you hear sirens.

BORN-AGAIN ANNE RICE

Looks like someone's been picking her nose! Okay, you have to
pinch it and lean forward. You're still swallowing blood? Now,
pack your nostrils with tissue to stuff it up. Good. So, have you
developed a taste for plasma? Congratulations, you've conquered
the test of a vampyre. Good news: you're not undead!

AQUA NET®

Don't forget, the surface of a pond or river may look frozen, but
the ice could still crack, and you can easily slip under. Why not
take up a nice indoor hobby, like owl macramé, whittling with a
steak knife or thousand-piece puzzling?

ATROPA BELLADONNA

Never take medicine without a responsible adult present. A health care professional would call that "self-mediating behaviour." But if you're really jonesing, ask a responsible adult. And even though your cousin calls himself a naturopath, he doesn't count. Don't take anything he gives you, no matter what he calls them. I'm talking no deadly nightshade, no Duo-Tang, no rusty jumper cables . . .

COPYRIGHTINFRINGEMENT

There's nothing chicken about being smart. Unless, of course, you're being kept in a cage while strangers steal all your eggs. Stopping to think about flying the coop won't make it easier to put up with. There's almost always a better way, but so long as the present administration subsidizes draconian factory farming practices this is as good as it gets for you. Stop wishing for good governance and chew your pellets. Don't make us get the force-feeding tube.

CHIRON

So, I see you're still swinging and missing, li'l slugger. Looks like you should either squint a lot or get a pair of spectacles. Of course, you could also try my home remedy: mix a poultice or salve from a dram of ammonia, a pint of day-old gruel and the ashes of the Union Jack. Place directly on eyes. Either that, or switch to softball. Meet your problem and beat it - with a bat!

MOTHER OF PEARL OF WISDOM

Running away from home won't solve your problems! Your mind will keep running long after your legs stop. Remember how the clam makes a pearl: it deposits layers of calcium carbonate over an irritant or particle. So, if you want to make a pearl of yourself, ruminate. It's not too late!

ROD SERLING'S OLDER SISTER

When you're playing hide-and-seek, never crawl inside anything that could close up and trap you. You don't want to get stuck like the memories of that time when your older brother said, "Submitted for your approval. There's a deserted chest freezer in the back alley! Want to play house, Judy?" Remember? You know, that time you and your brother found the autopsied alien?

ANNA OLD SOUL

If you chance upon a gentlewoman who has caught the vapours, espy whether she draws breath, even faintly. If she breathes, lay her on a chaise longue and loosen her corset. Ensure that hysteria has not set in by gently massaging her torso. If she is not hysterical, but the breath of life has left her, ensure her spirit will not linger by removing all other maidens from the premises. Poltergeists are known to anchor themselves upon passionate, chaotic feminine emotions.

SUPERHEROINE WOMAN GIRL

Contrary to popular belief, you don't get superpowers from surviving electrocution. All you get is third-degree burns, cardiac arrest or prolonged periods of unconsciousness. Try to keep your fingers out of wall sockets and your tongue away from exposed wires.

SALOME

Don't judge people 'til you give them a chance. Then, if they don't appreciate how many days of counting carbs or hours of rehearsal it took to pull off the forbidden dance of the seven veils for his fiftieth birthday bash, judge away! Hear that, Herod? Heads will roll!

BLINKING "12:00"

Remember, taking something that isn't yours just isn't right. Unless it's land from native people, clean air and water from future generations, collective bargaining rights from the working class or reproductive freedom from women. Nothing wrong with any of that! Oh no no no. Not one thing.

FEMME MORGAN LE FATALE

A stranger is anyone you don't know yet, right? That's why I wear my name, Morgan, here, on this tag. And right here is the name

(FEMME MORGAN LE FATALE, cont'd)

of the family restaurant chain that employs me as a server. The corporate entity whose logo appears on my paycheque kindly suggested that I not identify them by name. See, they are presently in court defending against a class action lawsuit. One word. Starts with *list*. Rhymes with *Bavaria*. I guess what I'm saying is that even though you know my employers by name, they're still kind of strangers, and dangerous ones at that. Could I interest you in a Grand Slam® breakfast?

TATTOO OF KANJI CHARACTER FOR FERTILITY

A haz-mat suit is good protection in an attic filled with asbestos – almost like a life jacket in a tippy canoe, a spacesuit on the dark side of the moon or a chastity belt in a Gothic manor. Good to know you're good to go!

CHLOË KARAOKE

No matter how many educational advisors you consult, consultants you coordinate or coordinators you advise, a public service announcement is only another sort of commercial. I mean, who do we think we're fooling? Ourselves – and only ourselves. We've long conditioned children to tune out the Skinner box during the advertisements.

CHECK YOUR LOCAL LISTINGS

11 **ALL RIGHTS RESERVED** – BW

12 **ASTRO BOY®S ERROR** – triolet

★★☆☆

Thomas Hardy structures "Birds at Winter Nightfall" (1899) to give you a feeling of déjà vu. Within its eight iambic (i.e., da-*dum*) lines, there are only two rhymes and two refrain lines (i.e., *abbabbaab*) to give you a feeling of déjà vu.

13 **ON PANELS WITH POMEGRANATES AND INSTRUMENTS OF MUSIC** – sestina ★★★★

For Mark Sampson. With "Farm Implements and Rutabagas in a Landscape" (1966), John Ashbery turns the sestina into a game – or maybe some sort of memory trick. The poem cycles through the same six words at the end of lines of six stanzas plus an envoi of three lines. The device is so nimbly mnemonic it doesn't even have to rhyme.

15 *LES SCHTROUMPFS*™

Based on "The Fish" by Marianne Moore (1918).

17 **CRUDE SCOOBY**™ – curtal sonnet

★★☆☆

Gerard Manley Hopkins shrinks the Petrarchan sonnet to three-quarter scale in "Pied Beauty" (1877; 1918), making ten and a half lines instead of fourteen, with a sextet (i.e., a six-line section) instead of an octave (i.e., an eight-line section) and a quatrain (i.e., a four-line section) instead of a sextet. Same number of rhymes, though (i.e., *abcabc dbcdc*). Hopkins called the rhythm of his poem "sprung," which roughly means that the number of strong stressed syllables per line varies.

18 **ROBOT WORK**

Unicron . . . . Orson Welles

20 **THE SCROOGE**

Based on "The Choice" by William Butler Yeats (1932).

21 **A TITLE BILLING** – blank verse

★★★☆

Yeats writes "The Second Coming" (1920) with regular metre – in this case iambic pentameter (i.e., ten beats per line) – but without regular rhymes. It seems like the poem hypnotizes you with the look of a swinging pocket watch and then snaps you awake. Aaand sleep. Bark like a rough beast!
Howard the Duck™ . . . . Himself

Look Closer . . . .

23 THE CHURCH OF ARCHIE

While working days for Archie® Comics, artist and writer Al Hartley moonlighted for Spire Christian Comics. Sometime in the late 1970s, Spire publisher Fleming H. Revell commissioned Hartley to spread the gospel around Riverdale High by creating an evangelical line of books. In it, the gang of high school Archie®-types preach the Good Word through adventures featuring holier-than-thou morals. Four of the issues are represented here in the form of a rime royale.

It takes five septets (i.e., seven-line stanzas) and four octaves for Auden to proclaim the glories of "The Shield of Achilles" (1952). But it's the scheme (i.e., *ababbcc*) that makes his rhymes royal.

Repeat. Published in *Dreamland*, ed. Jeremy Stewart.

26 PICTURE-IN-PICTURE – free verse
★★☆☆

W.H. Auden doesn't bother with a formulaic rhyme scheme or rhythm pattern in "Musée des Beaux Arts" (1939; 1940). Instead, he breaks the poem into two parts. The first strophe (i.e., movement) makes a statement about the art in the museum named in the title, but then the second strophe moves to a detail of one painting. That's why it's called an *ekphrastic* poem (i.e., a detailed description of an image). It almost seems as though the speaker's a little too worried about keeping up appearances.

27 LADY AND AN ELDER

Based on "Madam and the Minister" by Langston Hughes (1964). Repeat. Published on newpoetry.ca, ed. George Murray.

29 ODE TO MADONNA

For Jenessa Kehler. Based on "Ode to a Model" by Vladimir Nabokov (1955). Repeat. Published in *Train*, ed. D.W. Adams.

31 COUNTDOWN TO WATCHING *THUNDERBIRDS*™

Based on "Thirteen Ways of Looking at a Blackbird" by Wallace Stevens (1923; 1931). Repeat. Published on *Canadian Poetries*, ed. Kimmy Beach and Shawna Lemay.

34 THE EVENING CHANT OF A LOST LAND

Based on "Morning Song in the Jungle" by Rudyard Kipling (1895).

35 A VINCENTINE: TO HIM WHOSE NAME HAUNTS THE FOLLOWING LINES – acrostic ★★★☆

Edgar Allan Poe hides his beloved Frances Sargent Osgood's name within the lines of "A Valentine" (1849) – diagonally, from the first letter of the first line through the twentieth letter of the twentieth line. This isn't quite as charming as it would seem at first. Trapping her inside a poem is more than a little creepy. Inventor . . . . Vincent Leonard Price Jr.

36 AIRING AT NIGHT / PAYING AT MORNING

Based on "Meeting at Night" / "Parting at Morning" by Robert Browning (1845).

37 EXPLETYPOGRAPHY

For Jonathan Ball.

40 from AN ERA FOR ADVERTISING – alliterative tetrameter ★★☆☆

For Nikki Reimer and Jonathon Wilcke. A form as old as poetry itself, especially the Germanic kind, alliterative verse still sounds right. The effect of repeating a consonant sound about four times a line is almost subliminal. Auden knew this. The sounds of his long poem "An Age of Anxiety" (1947) are hard to get out of your head. Repeat. Published in *CV2*, eds. Sharanpal Ruprai and Jennifer Still.

42 THE TASTE OF SLIME – ottava rima ★☆☆☆

In *Byrne* (1995), Anthony Burgess designs rhymes in sections of eight lines (i.e., ababab*cc*) to weave a bawdy tale. Byron used it for grins – but, uh, groan.

43 ALTHOUGH SHE WOULD NOT CRUSH THE HORDE – ballad stanza ★★☆☆

Emily Dickinson has no truck with common metre – the da-*dum* rhythm is too strict, and the *abab* rhyme is too restrictive – so she trucks with it. The varying rhythms (i.e., switching between three and four *x*s per line) and rhymes (i.e., *abcb*) in "Because I could not stop for Death" (1890) strike an uncommon, almost uncanny, tone. Repeat. Published in *Geez*, ed. Melanie Dennis Unrau.

44 THE GREY TRANSFORMER™

Based on "The Red Wheelbarrow" by William Carlos Williams (1923).

45 ON THE FLOOR OF JCPENNEY®

Based on "In a Station of the Metro" by Ezra Pound (1916).

46 RUXPIN™

Based on "My Papa's Waltz" by Theodore Roethke (1948).

47 A HOOT

Based on "A Light" by Gertrude Stein (1939).

Look Closer . . . .

(48) OH! PORTMANTEAUS!

The US president launched the EPA at the end of 1970. The US military stopped dropping Agent Orange in Vietnam by 1971. That's some of the news Dr. Seuss™ was reading when he published his fable *The Lorax*. A creature of the forest, the eponymous Lorax stages a demonstration against the greedy head of a corporation who is processing the trees into clothing of some sort. The good doctor wrote the text in hopes of getting us talking about the environment. It worked.

"Ah! Sun-flower" by William Blake (1794) sounds almost Seussian. That's probably because Dr. Seuss wrote with the loopy rhythm (i.e., *da-da-dum*), pattern (i.e., four *xs* per line) and rhyme (i.e., *abab*) of Blake's anapestic tetrameter.

Repeat. Published in *AntiLang*, eds. Jordan Bolay and Allie McFarland.

(49) JABBERJAWKY

Based on "Jabberwocky" by Lewis Carroll (1871).

(50) KAPOWIEEE

Based on "Karawane" by Hugo Ball (1917).

(51) POWER GOES COMMANDO AFTER BOOT-⇧ – villanelle ★ ★ ★ ★

For Dina Del Beano. There's a code to Dylan Thomas's "Do Not Go Gentle into that Good Night" (1952). It's made of five tercets (i.e., three-line stanzas) that rhyme *aba* and one quatrain that rhymes *abaa*. It also repeats certain lines: the first line of the poem shows up as the last line of the second and the fourth tercet; the third line of the poem shows up as the last line of the third and the fifth tercet; the first line of the poem shows up as the second-last line of the quatrain; and the second line of the poem shows up as the last line. See kids: coding is easy! Repeat. Published in *Matrix*, ed. derek beaulieu.

(52) TYPE "C:\POOLRAD> START.EXE STING"

Based on "*In tausend Formen magst du dich verstecken*" by Johann Wolfgang von Goethe (German; 1815). Repeat. Published on *our teeth*, ed. kevin mcpherson eckhoff.

(54) *TETЯIS*™ EFFECT – (BW)

Repeat. Published in *filling Station*, ed. Weyman Chan.

Look Closer . . . .

⑤⑤ CHECKFORYARINDYORHSW EASTEREGG

Despite the rush to get the *E.T. the Extra-Terrestrial*® video game for Atari® 2600™ onto store shelves by Christmas 1983, developer Howard Scott Warshaw took precious moments to hide three messages about other video games he had previously programmed. (He already had a rep as the first e-Easter bunny.) Long-suffering players could find "Indy," the nickname of the archaeologist Indiana Jones™; "Yar," the name of the hero from *Yars' Revenge*®, or "HSW," initials of the name his parents chose. The lines of code in question appear here to accompany this rondel.

With "*Rien au réveil*" (French; 1885), Stéphane Mallarmé effectively reprogrammed a singsong round. Forgetting about standardized metre, he focused on two quatrains and a quintet (i.e., a five-line stanza). The first two lines are a refrain that repeat in the last two lines of the second and third stanzas.

Repeat. Published on *our teeth*, ed. kevin mcpherson eckhoff.

⑤⑥ LEVEL 256 – pantoum ★★★☆

Something like the villanelle, this form is made up of four quatrains that follow a scheme where the second and fourth lines of one stanza serve as the first and third lines of the next. Also, the third line of the first stanza becomes the second last line of the poem and the first line of the poem becomes the last line of the poem. This kind of tongue-twisting looks easy in Charles

Baudelaire's "*Harmonie du soir*" (French; 1857). Repeat. Published in *Poetry is Dead*, ed. Cynara Geissler.

⑤⑧ YOU WILL KNOW IT'S TIME TO TURN THE PAGE WHEN YOU HEAR THE CHIMES RING (CC)

Published on *our teeth*, ed. kevin mcpherson eckhoff. Original airdate: 15 November 2016.

⑥⓪ SCHOOLHOUSE ____! (CC)

Repeat. Published in *experiment-o*, ed. Amanda Earl.

⑥④ WARNING REGARDING *CARE BEARS*™

After Hilaire Belloc.

⑥⑤ BOB BROADCASTS BANKRUPT BEAUTY BOOB BY BOOB – Shakespearean sonnet ★★☆☆

A.k.a. Elizabethan or English. A robust sort of sonnet, the three quatrains and couplet (i.e., two-line section) use a steady rhyme scheme (i.e., *abab cdcd efef gg*). This construction is virtually indestructible. Only it and the cockroaches will survive nuclear annihilation. This one is modelled on Robert Frost's "Never Again Would Birds' Song Be the Same" (1942).

66 PROTOCOL

After Robert Pinsky.

67 DROIDS™

After Robert Lowell. Repeat. Published on *Poemeleon*, ed. rob mclennan.

68 HEARING THE WEEKLY SECRET LETS ME SCREAM

After Edna St. Vincent Millay.

69 SNARF™

After Seamus Heaney.

70 THROUGH GOLDEN AGES GIRLS LODGE TOGETHER

For Danny Zomps. After John Keats.

71 HULK HOGAN'S 24" PYTHONS

After Rainer Maria Rilke.

72 *KNIGHT RIDER*™

After Christina Rossetti.

73 MAJESTY

After Gertrude Stein.

74 SPOCK™S SPOKEN-WORD TRACKS

For Moribund Facekvetch. After Matthew Arnold.

75 MILLI VANILLI

After Percy Bysshe Shelley. Repeat. Published in *PRISM international*, ed. Shazia Hafiz Ramji.

76 McDONALDLAND™: COMMERCIAL POEM

After Ralph Waldo Emerson.

77 SONNET N – Petrarchan sonnet
★★☆☆

A.k.a. Italian. An ornate sort of sonnet, the octave (i.e., eight-line section) and sestet use a stable rhyme scheme (i.e., *abbaabba cdecde*). The intricacy of this structure is crystalline. Hit an operatic frequency and see what happens to the poem. (Hint: it shatters.) This one is patterned after John Berryman's "Sonnet 13" (1969).

78 COSBY SONNET

After Elizabeth Bishop.

79 *CENTIPEDE*™

After John Ashbery.

80 ELOQUENCE QUA MYSTIQUE –
terza rima ★ ☆ ☆ ☆

This scheme uses a rhyme chain, where the second line of one tercet rhymes with the first and third line of the next (i.e., *aba bcb*, etc.). Dante did it best, but he wrote with a fine Italian hand, so this poem follows Frost's example.

81 CARTOON BUTTERFLY

After Gwendolyn Brooks.

82 THIGHMASTER™

After Elizabeth Barrett Browning.

83 THIS TV SPOT

After T.S. Eliot.

84 PEGASUS

After Paul Muldoon. Repeat. Published on *Poemeleon*, ed. rob mclennan.

85 VIDEOTAPES

After Adrienne Rich.

86 WONDER

For Caley Ehnes. After Amy Lowell. Repeat. Published in *Lemon Hound 3.0*, ed. Jake Byrne.

87 *SUPER*BETAMAX®

After Ted Berrigan.

88 TOUCHY CLAY

After Arthur Rimbaud.

89 CANONIZE ZELLERS

After Hart Crane.

90 NOW YOU KNOW, AND KNOWING MAKES YOU A SUPERSTAR!

Repeat. Published on *Crap Orgasm*, ed. A.G. Pasquella. Original airdate: 7 March 2017.

ACKNOWLEDGEMENTS

Thanks to Paul Vermeersch for getting it (and, in a way, getting me).

Thanks to Noelle Allen, Ashley Hisson, Jared Shapiro and the good people at Wolsak & Wynn.

Thanks to Sharon for always understanding.

To friends who share their lives with me, thank you; to family who had no choice but to share their lives with me, thank you, too.

Thanks, also, to you – yes, you – for reading, and for sitting through it to the end.

nathan dueck's middle name is russel, which means his initials spell *nrd*. His folks tell him that nobody used that word when he was born, but dictionaries say otherwise. He is the author of *king's(mère)* (Turnstone Press) and *he'll* (Pedlar Press). Born in Winnipeg, he completed his Ph.D. at the University of Calgary and now lives in Cranbrook, BC, where he is a creative writing and English instructor at the College of the Rockies.

AVSE now brings the day's poetic activities
to an end.

AVSE broadcasts in these pages,
between 210 to 216 MHz,
with a maximum radiated
power of 316,000 watts video
and 39,000 watts audio.

AVSE invites you to join us
at the regularly scheduled time
for another day of the finest
in varied entertainment
and information programming.

Until then, on behalf of
the author and publisher of *AVSE*,
good night, everyone.

In closing, let us observe
a moment of patriotic
reflection . . .

ead air d   dead air de
air dead ai   air dead air dead air de
de air air de   dead air dead air dead air dead ai   ad air dead air dead air dea
ir dead a   r dead   air dead air dead air dead air dea   ead air dead air dead air dead air de
ad air   air ead air dead air dead air dead air dead air dead ai   ead air dead air dead air dead air d
r dead r dead air dead air dead air dead air dead air dead air dea   air dead air dead air dead air dead air
ad air ad air dead air dead air dead air dead air dead air dead ai dead air dead air dead air dead air dea
ir dead air dead air dead air dead air dead air dead air dead air dea air dead air dead air dead air dead air
ead air dead air dead air dead air dead air dead air dead air dead ai dead air dead air dead air dead air dead
r dead ir dead air dead air dead air dead air dead air dead air dea air dead air dead air dead air dead air
ad air ead air dead air dead air dead air dead air dead air dead ai dead air dead air dead air dead air dead
r dead ir dead air dead air dead air dead air dead air dead air dea air dead air dead air dead air dead air
ad air ead air dead air dead air dead air dead air dead air dead ai dead air dead air dead air dead air dead
r dead ir dead air dead air dead air dead air dead air dead air dea air dead air dead air dead air dead air
ad air ead air dead air dead air dead air dead air dead air dead ai dead air dead air dead air dead air dead
r dead ir dead air dead air dead air dead air dead air dead air dea air dead air dead air dead air dead air
ad air ead air dead air dead air dead air dead air dead air dead ai dead air dead air dead air dead air dead
r dead ir dead air dead air dead air dead air dead air dead air dea air dead air dead air dead air dead air
ad air ead air dead air dead air dead air dead air dead air dead ai dead air dead air dead air dead air dead
r dead ir dead air dead air dead air dead air dead air dead air dea air dead air dead air dead air dead air
ad air ead air dead air dead air dead air dead air dead air dead ai dead air dead air dead air dead air dead
r dead ir dead air dead air dead air dead air dead air dead air dea air dead air dead air dead air dead air
ad air ead air dead air dead air dead air dead air dead air dead ai dead air dead air dead air dead air dead
r dead ir dead air dead air dead air dead air dead air dead air dea air dead air dead air dead air dead air
ad air ead air dead air dead air dead air dead air dead air dead ai dead air dead air dead air dead air dead
r dead ir dead air dead air dead air dead air dead air dead air dea air dead air dead air dead air dead air
ad air ead air dead air dead air dead air dead air dead air dead ai d dead air dead air dead air dead air dead
r dead ir dead air dead air dead air dead air dead air dead ai   r dea air dead air dead air dead air dead air
ad air ead air dead air dead air dead air dead air ad air de d ai dead air dead air dead air dead air dead
r dead ir dead air dead air dead a   air dead air dea air dead air   air dead air
ad air ead air dead air de   dead air dead ai dead ai   air dead
ir dead air dead air   air dead air d d a   air
ead air dead a   ad air de   e
r dead ir
ad air e
r dead